Football Clones

Contents

Football Clones

Brandon Robshaw

Published in association with
The Basic Skills Agency

Hodder & Stoughton

A MEMBER OF THE HOD⋯

Acknowledgements
Cover: Dave Hopkins
Illustrations: Dave Hopkins

Orders: please contact Bookpoint Ltd, 78 Milton Park, Abingdon, Oxon OX14
4TD. Telephone: (44) 01235 827720, Fax: (44) 01235 400454. Lines are open
from 9.00–6.00, Monday to Saturday, with a 24-hour message answering service.
Email address: orders@bookpoint.co.uk

British Library Cataloguing in Publication Data
A catalogue record for this title is available from The British Library

ISBN 0 340 80234 0

First published 2001
Impression number   10 9 8 7 6 5 4 3 2 1
Year   2007 2006 2005 2004 2003 2002 2001

Typeset by SX Composing DTP, Rayleigh, Essex.
Printed in Great Britain for Hodder & Stoughton Educational, a division of
Hodder Headline Plc, 338 Euston Road, London NW1 3BH, by Athenaeum
Press, Gateshead, Tyne & Wear.

1

A Big Day

'It's the big day today!' said Paul.
He picked up a piece of toast and bit into it.
Robbie, the robot, poured him a cup of tea.
'Thanks, Robbie.
Yes, it's the big one today.'

Paul's father looked up
from his electronic newspaper.
'What are you talking about?'

'The scout's coming!' said Paul.

'The scout?' said Paul's mother.
'You mean a boy scout?'

'No, Mum!
I mean a football scout.
The scout for Manchester Allstars!'

Paul's dad switched off
his electronic newspaper.
'The scout for Manchester Allstars?
Coming to your school?
Why didn't you tell us before?'

'Mr Scott only told us yesterday,' said Paul.
'Then last night I was out, wasn't I?
Training with Hackney FC.'

'If Manchester Allstars pick you,
you won't be playing for Hackney
much longer!'

'Wouldn't that be cool!' said Paul.
'I must have a chance.
I'm top scorer for Hackney this season.'

'That's non-league stuff, though,'
said Paul's dad.
'Manchester Allstars are a massive club.
They've got the clones of Pele
and George Best and Maradona
playing for them.'

'Just imagine,' said Paul.
'Me playing with Pele
and Best and Maradona.'

'Don't get your hopes up,' said Paul's mother.
'They must see thousands of schoolboys.
And they don't sign many.
You think too much about football, you do.'

'Oh, Mum!
How can anyone think too much
about football?'

'You should think more
about your school work.
Look at the time!
You're going to be late for school.
Get into that transporter now.'

'Your mother's right,' said Paul's dad.
'You don't want to be late for the scout.'

'OK, OK,' said Paul.
He finished his tea.
He picked up his football kit.
'Wish me luck,' he said.

'Good luck,' said his father.
Paul stepped into the transporter –
a large glass box by the door.
He pressed the button.
There was a humming noise
and a bright light.

Paul disappeared from sight.

2

Paul and David

The entrance hall to Paul's school
was full of transporters.
The humming noise was everywhere.
Bright lights flashing all around.
People stepping out of glass boxes
wherever you looked.
Paul saw his best friend, David.
They both played for Hackney FC.
'Hey, Paul! Big day today.'

'Too right,' said David.
'You nervous?'

'A bit. You?'

'Yeah, a bit.'

6

'It'd be cool if we both got picked.
Just imagine –
being a professional footballer!
Getting paid for something you love doing.'

'Yeah,' said David.
'And playing for Manchester Allstars –
the biggest club in Britain.'

'Being in the same team
as Pele and Best and Maradona,' said Paul.

'Well, their clones, anyway,' said David.

'Same thing,' said Paul.

'If they sign, they'll make clones
of you, too,' said David.

'I know,' said Paul.
'That's cool.
I'll still be able to watch myself playing
fifty years from now.'

Mr Scott, the PE teacher,
came into the hall in his tracksuit.
'All right, boys.
Time to calm down and get ready.
The scout's already here.
Anyone who's played
for the first or second team,
get changed and out on the pitch.'

3

The Game of His Life

Paul ran out on to the field.
It was a bright autumn day.
The sky was blue, the grass was green.
Paul loved this moment.
In a world of clones and computers
and transporters and robots,
it was good just to run out on a field
and play football.
Just like people had done
for the last two hundred years.

Paul felt fit and on form.
He was ready to play the game of his life.
He looked at the scout – a small man in a hat,
standing on the touch line.

Mr Scott blew the whistle.
Paul's team kicked off.
Paul ran into space, calling for the ball.
The ball was passed to him.
He took it up the wing, beating two players.
He banged in a perfect cross.
David headed it but it flew just over the bar.

Time and time again,
Paul found space and made things happen.
He made his team's first goal.
Then, just before half time,
he ran up the wing, cut inside
and shot from the edge of the box.

It was a beautiful, hard, low shot.
The goalkeeper had no chance.
The ball crashed into the corner of the net.

Paul was playing the game of his life.
You could see that he loved the game.
He was doing what he did best.
In the second half, he ran the game.
He scored twice more.
Even the scout clapped his last goal,
a clever lob over the goalie's head.

Mr Scott blew the whistle for full time.
The score was 4–1 to Paul's team.
'Well done, man!' said David.
'You were great.'

'You played OK, too,' said Paul.
David hadn't played badly.
But not as well as Paul.
Paul was Man of the Match.
There was no doubt about that.

Mr Scott came over to him.
'Paul,' he said,
'the scout would like a word with you.'

4

'Yes!'

'I like the way you play,' said the scout.
He was quite an old man.
He had a red face and sharp blue eyes.
'You've got a lot of skill
and I can see you really love the game.'

'Thanks,' said Paul.

'We might be interested,' said the scout.
'We might be interested in signing you.'

Paul couldn't believe it.
It was a dream come true.
'Yes!' he shouted.

The scout smiled.
'Don't get too excited yet.
We'll have to give you a trial first
and carry out a medical check.
We'll also have to clone you.
We'll need your parents' consent for that.'

'That won't be a problem,' said Paul.

'Right,' said the scout.
'Well, we'll be in touch with your parents.
We'll arrange for you to come and train
with the big boys next week.'
He put out his hand. Paul shook it.
'Thanks,' he said.

Paul ran back to the changing room.
He felt as if he was flying.
'Well?' said David. 'What did he say?'

'Yes!' shouted Paul.
'If I do OK at the trial, they'll sign me.'

'Well done!' said David. 'You deserve it.'
He tried to smile but he looked a bit sad.
'I guess you won't be playing
for Hackney FC any more.'

'I guess not,' said Paul.

5

The Trial

Paul's parents were surprised
and pleased at the news.
Especially Paul's dad.
'I knew you could do it!' he said.

The trial was a week later.
Paul's mum and dad went to watch.
They went in the transporter.

Paul's parents sat in the stand,
next to Jock Robinson, the Allstars manager.

Paul changed and ran out on to the field.
He had butterflies in his stomach.
He saw Pele and Best and Maradona
knocking the ball around.
Well, their clones, anyway.
It was amazing.
They were legends.
They'd played way before Paul was born.
Yet here they were,
knocking the ball around, as large as life.

Paul was on Pele's side.
The trainer blew the whistle.
The match began.

It was hard for Paul at first.
The game was much faster and tougher
than he was used to.
The players were much more skilful.
He couldn't get the ball off them.

As the game went on, Paul got used to it.
He got into his stride.
He made a few tackles.
He made a few passes.
He had a shot that went just wide.

He knew he was playing well.
He started to enjoy himself.
He didn't score,
but he got involved in some very good moves.
Just before the end,
he found space on the wing
and made one of his perfect crosses.
Pele rose and headed it into the net.
Goal!

Paul's mum and dad clapped.
Pele raised his hand to Paul.
'Well done,' he said. 'Good cross.'

Paul couldn't believe it.
Pele, the great Pele,
had said 'Well done' to him!

6

'Sign here, please'

After the match, Paul and his parents
were called to Jock Robinson's office.
'Coffee?' said Jock Robinson.
A robot brought it in.
'Cigar?'
He gave one to Paul's dad and lit one himself.
'Not for you, laddie,' he said to Paul.
'You've got to keep yourself fit.
You did well today.
I was impressed with your performance.'

'Thanks,' said Paul.

'I've had the results of your medical,'
said Robinson.
'You're a fit, healthy laddie.
Good muscle structure.
You'll not be getting injured often.'

'That's good to hear,' said Paul's mother.

'In short, laddie,' said Jock Robinson,
'I've decided to sign you.
Here's the contract.
Have a look at it.
Standard cloning clause, of course.
Signing fee of fifty million.
Salary of twenty million a year.'

Paul's parents looked at the contract.
'It looks fine,' said Paul's dad.

'That's grand,' said Jock Robinson.
'Sign here, please.'

7

'Just a minute...'

'Just a minute,' said Paul.
'Can I ask something?'

'Of course you can, laddie.'

'This cloning clause – what's it all about?'

'It gives us the right to make
as many clones of you as we need.
And they'll be under contract to play for us.'

'And they get paid, do they?'

'They're looked after.
Don't worry about that.
Your twenty million is safe, laddie.'

'It's not that,' said Paul.
'It's just – who are you signing, really?
Me, or my clone?'

'Let me explain,' said Jock Robinson.
'A clone is a copy of you.
We can make a clone from any cell
of your body.
It's like a kind of twin –
except that it's younger than you.
It will be a baby to start with, you see?
By the time it's grown up and ready,
you'll be too old to play.'

'OK – but until then it's me that plays, right?'

Jock Robinson scratched his chin.
'I have to tell you, it's unlikely.
It's unlikely we'd need you to play, as such.
A team with the likes of
Pele and Best and Maradona in it –
well, you can't just walk into it,
you'll understand.
But your clone – we'll be training him up
from a baby to fit into the team.
By the time he's eighteen,
he'll be just ready, do you see?
It's a long-term plan.
Now, if you'll sign here...'

'Just a minute,' said Paul.
'If I can't play for you, I can play
for other teams, right?
You see, I play for this non-league team,
Hackney FC...'

Jock Robinson scratched his head.
'I can hear what you're saying, laddie.
I have to tell you, we couldn't permit you
to play for another team.
Even a non-league team.
It would break the contract, do you see?
In that event,
we wouldn't have to pay you anything.'

'Just a minute,' said Paul.
'So you're saying, if I sign for you,
I won't be able to play football ever again?'

'Well, not as your own self,'
said Jock Robinson.
'But your clone will be playing for us,
and your clone's the same as you...'

'Forget it,' said Paul.
He got up from his chair.

'Paul!' said his mother.
'Just think about this.'

'Don't do anything hasty,' said his father.
'You can't turn your back
on that sort of money!'

'Can't I?' said Paul,
and he walked out of the office.

8

'I don't believe it!'

'I don't believe it, man!' said David.
'You turned down Manchester Allstars.'

'That's right,' said Paul.
It was Saturday.
Paul and David were walking
to Hackney FC's ground for the game.

'You turned down fifty million quid!'
said David.
'And a salary of twenty million!'

'That's right,' said Paul.

'You must be crazy!'

'I'm not crazy,' said Paul.
'I just love football.'

They reached the ground.
They got changed.
'Let's play football,' said Paul.

Paul ran out on to the field.
It was a bright autumn day.
The sky was blue, the grass was green.
Paul loved this moment.
In a world of clones and computers
and transporters and robots,
it was good just to run out on a field
and play football.
Just like people had done
for the last two hundred years.